THIS WALKER BOOK BELONGS TO:

For Max

First published 1982 by Evans Brothers Ltd
This edition published 1991 Walker Books Ltd
87 Vauxhall Walk, London SE11 5HJ

Reprinted 1992

© 1982 Colin Hawkins

Printed and bound in Hong Kong by
Sheck Wah Tong Printing Press Ltd

British Library Cataloguing in Publication Data
Hawkins, Colin
How to look after your dog.
I. Title
823'.914 [J]
ISBN 0-7445-2079-7

HOW TO LOOK AFTER YOUR DOG

Colin Hawkins

WALKER BOOKS
LONDON

A dog is...

A dog is furry with four legs, a tail that wags and a cold wet nose.

"And sharp teeth."

A dog is someone who is able to hear a can being opened from down the end of the garden...

"I do like fires."

"Sounds like dinner time."

Someone to share the fire with.

A dog is someone
who loves you ...

Someone to share
the sofa with.

A dog is someone to bring your
slippers, or the newspapers,
or his favourite old sock,
or his old bone...

Choice of Dog

A dog is a friend that you can choose – though often he will choose you.

Don't take away a puppy who is too young and hasn't been weaned yet.

Pick a lively, happy puppy with bright eyes and a glossy coat.

shine
shine
gleam
gleam

This is to certify that Rover has been inoculated against distemper, hard pad, soft pad, toad in the hole.

Before he leaves the kennel make sure that your pup has been given his inoculations.

"Is it dinner-time yet?"

In choosing your dog make sure that you pick the right dog for your home and pocket.

Please help. Large dog to feed.

First Night Home

On his first night away from the
kennels a puppy can be lonely.
Wrap a hot water bottle in a
blanket and place it in his
basket. An alarm clock can
also be a comfort.

(Don't forget to switch off the alarm.)

On his first arrival home be
careful how your new
pup is introduced to
older and more
established pets.

"Whose dinner are you?"

"Hello, sir."

Even if he is lonely on his first night home, it is not a good idea to allow a pup to sleep on your bed...

This can lead to problems as he grows up – especially if he grows and grows.

Diet

When your puppy is ready to be weaned, usually around eight weeks, gradually begin to introduce a meat-based diet.

A growing dog will eat almost anything from "Tiddles" choice fish bits to carpet slippers and other people's dinners.

One good meal a day should be enough for any dog.

A balanced diet should consist of meat, fish, brown bread, vegetables, biscuits and table left-overs (or table left-unders).

Too much raw meat will make a dog's breath smell.

"Hello, Rover"

"What a nasty niff!"

bone china

Tea

Dogs can also enjoy tea, although tea-drinking dogs
are usually found only in the British Isles.

Do not over-feed your dog or you will end up taking him for a roll rather than a walk.

How to recognize an overweight dog

a persistent beggar

excessive dribbling

fatty rounded chest

flabby belly

"More ...
please ...
more ...
more ...
please..."

roll of fat on his back

Remember
Your dog will get as fat as you allow him.

Toilet-training

All dogs need to be
toilet-trained.
Introduce your pup to
his litter-tray on his
first day home.

And then encourage the habit of going
outside as soon as possible.

When in town, train your
dog to use
the gutter.

Allowing a dog to foul the pavement is an offence. Dog-fouled pavements are unsightly, a health hazard and can be dangerous.

Pavement Fouler

"Oops, sorry!"

Don't allow your dog to foul places where children play. This can cause a very serious health hazard.

Obedience

"Oh, I do like walkies."

It is very important, in order for both
you and your dog to enjoy a happy life together,

that he should be obedient at all times.

"Well ... I did like walkies..."

Obedience Training

Sit
To teach your dog to "sit" press his tail-end gently but firmly to the ground at the same time telling him to "sit". When he has sat, praise and reward him.

Stay
When he understands "sit", teach him to "stay" by repeating the commands "sit" and "stay" while slowly backing away from him.

Good Boy!

Sit.

Sit."

"Good Boy!

"Hurry up, this grass is wet!"

"Stay ...

sit ...

stay ...

sit ...

stay.

Heel

Keeping the lead short, walk forwards slowly, pacing step-by-step with him. Whenever he begins to pull ahead, tug gently on the lead and say "heel". If he persists in pulling, stop and begin again.

Always praise him for getting it right.

Grooming

A dog's fur can at any time be full of fleas, twigs, ants, crumbs, old chewing gum or grass cuttings. Regular grooming is therefore essential.

"Left a bit..."

"Who's a pretty boy then?"

Bathing

"Baths are OK once you're in."

Give your dog a bath only in very warm weather. If he is so dirty that he has to be bathed during the winter, make sure that the room is very warm.

After his bath keep him well wrapped up in towels until he is totally dry.

Breeding
(The patter of tiny paws)

You must decide whether or not
you want your dog or bitch
to breed. There are several way
of preventing puppies. Ask
your vet for advice.

Keep your bitch
inside while she is on
heat in order to prevent unwanted
litters. And be prepared for unexpected callers.

If your bitch is going to have puppies and she begins spending more and more time in dark, quiet places, then the birth of her puppies is very near.

"Boo!"

Take care to see that her feeding bowls are close by and that the bed is comfortable and large enough for both her and the puppies. Try to avoid disturbing her and discourage visitors as much as you can.

Habits

A dog is a creature of habit...

He will instinctively join other dogs
and form a hunting pack.

"Hello, pack leader."

"...?? I thought you were pack leader!"

When your dog rolls over on his back, or crawls
along on his belly in front of you or another dog,
he is instinctively playing a submissive role
to the pack leader.

When he rolls in all the smelliest things he can find it is to camouflage his scent for hunting.

"What do you think of this fantastic camouflage smell, pack leader?"

"Ugh!"

"Round and round the garden..."

He will turn round and round in his basket to tread down the reeds as his ancestors did.

"Walkies, Bruce?"

"Ooh yes, please."

"Ooh yes!"

"Oh I do like walkies!"

He will also get very excited at being shown his lead, treating it as a signal from the pack leader (you) to work himself up into a pre-hunt fever.

Old Dogs

"Sit!"

"Yes, I am fit, thank you."

Old dogs can become
hard of hearing,
shortsighted and forgetful.

"Te ... tum ... te ... tum..."

Don't expect an old dog to walk too far. You may have to carry him home.

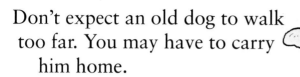

"The old legs aren't what they were."

"Mmm ... beef puree."

Chop food up as finely as possible.

Old dogs feel the cold more than young dogs, so keep them warm.

MORE WALKER PAPERBACKS
For You to Enjoy

Also by Colin & Jacqui Hawkins

How to Look After Your Cat

"Full of common sense and information, but a great laugh and even the most serious
advice has lovely drawings to go with it." *Sunday Magazine*
ISBN 0-7445-2078-9 £1.99

Farmyard Sounds / Jungle Sounds

"Lots of jolly cartoon-style animals… Every child I've ever known loves making animal noises,
so be prepared to do your stuff." *Tony Bradman, Parents*
Farmyard Sounds 0-7445-1752-4 £3.99
Jungle Sounds 0-7445-1753-2 £3.99

Terrible Terrible Tiger / The Wizard's Cat

Two wonderfully entertaining rhyming picture books about a tiger who is not
quite what he seems and a cat who wishes he were something else.
Terrible Terrible Tiger 0-7445-1063-5 £3.99
The Wizard's Cat 0-7445-1389-8 £2.99

**Walker Paperbacks are available from most booksellers, or by post from
Walker Books Ltd, PO Box 11, Falmouth, Cornwall TR10 9EN.**

To order, send: title, author, ISBN number and price for each book ordered, your full name and address
and a cheque or postal order for the total amount, plus postage and packing:
UK and BFPO Customers – £1.00 for first book, plus 50p for the second book and
plus 30p for each additional book to a maximum charge of £3.00.
Overseas and Eire Customers – £2.00 for first book, plus £1.00 for the second book and
plus 50p per copy for each additional book.
Prices are correct at time of going to press, but are subject to change without notice.